The Truth of Us

By: Cody McLendon

Cody McLendon was born on April 19, 1987 in Montgomery Alabama. Born and raised in Alabama, he is your normal "southern boy" at heart.

"The Truth of Us" is to represent, help, and encourage our LGBTQ about being true to themselves. There are daily struggles, issues, and hatred in the world. The only thing for you, is to be yourself and accept yourself. You owe that to you.

Coming out is a life – long process, not just a single event, which can begin at any age. Included with coming out there are many stages, and the fear or hatred that comprises homophobia. No two "coming out's" are the same, but you must start with yourself.

I hope this book can help anyone who is struggling to accept their sexuality, speak to parents of whom just had a child come out to them. I hope you can find it informative to use on your journey of being you.

With Love,

Cody McLendon

1

The Truth of Us, Identity Confusion. Who am I? With identity confusion, who am I is the biggest question of all. This is something that we spend not just minutes on. This is not like being a kid and one second wanting to be a police officer and the next second wanting to be a teacher. Deciding if regular Oreo's or Double Stuffed Oreo's are better. This is something on a much larger scale. Many of us spend years trying to figure all of this out, trying to understand the feelings that we are having towards someone, the way that our mind is telling us to feel about a certain person.

The biggest question I notice that people get asked when they come out is, "when did you know?" I'm not a fan of that question for one big reason. A part of me feels like we always know, we just don't want to accept it. Now I'm not saying my mother gave birth to me and I was in the new born section of the hospital checking out another baby, but what I am saying, growing up, you know. You always know there is something different about you.

So, let me answer the question. I guess I "knew" in or around fifth or sixth grade. Young you think? Not at all. Now a day's people are accepting the fact that they are gay, lesbian, bisexual, or transgender at younger ages, because the world is a changing place. Now just because I knew in or around the fifth or sixth grade, doesn't mean that I acted on it. That is not the case at all. I had just accepted the fact that I was different than those around me. I was finding myself looking at guys instead of the girls. I was more attracted to guys than girls.

Now I did have girlfriends…… two to be exact. I honestly still love both of those girls. They will always hold a special place in my heart. But let me explain, I went to a private school. A school that had grades K-4 to 12th grade, with a total enrollment of around 350 students. So, it was a very small school. Anybody who was anyone played football or cheered. First of all, I know nothing about sports, other than my mother makes a killer cheese dip when it is time for the Iron Bowl, I mean we are in the South. But I'm the type of guy who can't tell you the difference between a touchdown, field goal, homerun, or getting a basket (or whatever ya'll call it). Secondly, cheerleading was out of the question. I have not one ounce of rhythm in my body and have stage fright something serious. Plus, at a small school, cheerleading was for the girls. If a guy dared to join the cheer squad, that's just rumor's getting ready to happen. What would that rumor be? "He joined the cheer quad, well he must be gay!" Well yea, I am gay, but I'm not ready for everyone to know this just yet.

Going to such a small school, you look around, and you do nothing but judge yourself. You think to yourself that you are the only one like this at the school. I mean there are one or two that you assume, but you would never just ask, because like yourself, you're still trying to figure it all out. So that lead me to where all of my friends in school were females. I always got along way better with them. First, they're amazing. Second, they don't drool over sports all day. I had nothing in common with the guys at school and I damn sure wasn't going to fake something to make a friend. But the females, goodness, I just always had more in common and enjoyed everything that they liked to do. There were times where guys would get so mad at their girlfriend for always talking to Cody or hanging out with Cody. They would be so jealous. I mean boo, I'm just me. I'm wanting to scream "I'M GAY" at them, so get your testosterone under control, but that goes back to I'm not ready to announce that just yet. I watch the news and I live in the south, if I was to just announce that, well that scared the shit out of me. Here's this football player who is jealous over me because I talk with his girlfriend. So, let me just scream "I'M GAY" at him and take a chance of getting my ass kicked because he doesn't agree with my sexuality, or then I start getting accused of having feeling towards him. I'm not ready for that drama. So, I will just risk being friends with his girlfriend and taking an ass kicking over jealously rather than hatred. Thankfully, that never happened. The girls always defended me. "We are just friends!". They would take up constantly for me. Deep down, I knew they knew, but it was something that we didn't speak of. I never mentioned it to them because I wasn't ready, and none of them ever asked because of respect. They all loved me for me, and I am forever grateful for all of them.

Senior year and graduation, I was still in the closet. I was still not comfortable for my family, friends, or the world to know who I was. I was still figuring it out on my terms, and still trying to accept it myself. I was in a relationship throughout high school, a "secret relationship", with someone who did not go to my school. We dated from 9th grade till right after we graduated due to him moving away to college and everything. He was out to his family, but again, I wasn't ready. Was this who I really was or was this just a phase that I was going through?

The Trust of Us, Identity Confusion, my advice to you. Be yourself. Accept the fact that you are different, and you own that. Don't let nobody bring you down. Don't be scared. As I had to tell myself, there may a lot of hatred in this world, but if you open your eyes just a little more, you'll experience a lot more love. There are many resources available now to help our youth LGBTQ community, act on those resources. You deserve nothing more than to be yourself, but you can't be yourself until you accept yourself fully.

Now, parents. Pay attention. That is all we are wanting you to do, is just pay attention to us. This is the single most hardest thing that we will ever encounter in life, so we need you there for us when the time comes that we decide to tell you. It may be hard for you to accept it at first, or to understand it. But as your child, we will be needing you more in the moment that we tell you, than in any moment before that. Just remember, you are our parent and we are still your child.

2

The Truth of Us, Identity Comparison. Identity Comparison is when a person is trying to find an explanation for why they are having the feelings that they are experiencing. You may start feeling isolated, because you have so much going through your mind. You are going to question everything that goes through your mind. Is this a phase? Am I gay? Am I bisexual? Is this permanent? Let your mind do its wondering and you follow its lead. There is absolutely nothing wrong with any of those questions and don't let anybody answer those questions for you. It is up to you to find your true self and be who you are. Nobody else can make you, you.

When going through all of these questions and trying to find out about your true self, it is true that you may feel isolated. My advice, it's going to be isolated, to discover yourself, and take the time to come to terms with who you are. On that, never let yourself get into a "dark isolation" over it. An LGBTQ youth is 4 times more prone to attempting suicide than a heterosexual youth. I feel a majority of this comes from thoughts or guilt of that if anyone finds out, you are going to be unaccepted in this world. This is the farthest thing from the truth. Again, yes, you are going to run into hatred somewhere down the line, but you can not let that scare you off from being your true self. You brush it on, keep your chin up, and keep on going.

If you ever feel that your going into a dark isolation, seek help immediately. I will not be able to tell you that enough. There is a great organization out there for LGBTQ Youth called, The Trevor Project. This is a 24/7 organization that is available by phone, chat, and email. If you are ever feeling not worthy or just need to talk, reach out to them. Their counselors are the best out there and will help you through what it is that you are feeling.

I admit, I myself have been into the dark isolation a total of 2 times. It was scary, but I got help and got out of it.

The first time, I was living alone, I was 21 years old. I was still not out to most of the family and friends. By 20 years old, I had told a total of three people who I really was. So, I'm home alone and had a bad day. The thoughts of not feeling accepted, thoughts of me being 20 years old and still not 100% accepting this, and the thoughts of not being true to who I was. It wasn't just a one-night thing, it was a matter of months of thoughts and questions that had just got to be to much for me to handle. So, I remember it was around 10pm at night, I filled my bath tub up with water, and I had every intention of drowning myself that night. As I am getting ready to take my life, making sure I'm properly dressed, making sure there is a letter to my mom apologizing and explaining, my cellphone rings. It was my cousins boyfriend, so I answered it. He said to me "something told me to call you because we need to go riding tonight and just talk, I'm about 5 minutes away from you house so come outside and let's go." I instantly snapped out of it. I got in his car and we went cruising back roads, just talking about life.

So, then he hits me with "what was up with you tonight?" I'm all like, "what are you talking about?". He said, "Cody you are the quickest replier to a text that I've ever met, and before I called you, I had texted two hours before that and I never received a reply." It was with him saying that, I opened up about what was really going to happen that night.

A couple of years later, in between December and February, I started feeling myself going through the same things. It was Valentine's Day that year and instead of doing anything stupid, I just went to my primary care doctor and spoke to him. At this point, my mom knew I was gay, because my brother and sister n law went out with my mom and dad one night, so I just told them to tell them. It would keep me out of the hot seat and awkward questions that I don't like answering. Because I'm one of those people who don't like being put in a hot seat. But back on subject, I went to my primary care doctor. While I was there, he's asking questions about everything and I just have an emotional melt down in his office. So, he gives me two choices 1) I can call my mom while I'm sitting there with him and get her to come pick me up and take me to the hospital or 2) he would call the paramedics and have me transported, but I not to leave by myself. So, I chose to call my mom and try to inform her what was going on. Of course, when you are on the phone with someone who cares about you, it's hard to get all the words out, so my Doctor just puts his hand out for my phone. I give it to him, and he explains everything to my mother. Within 10 minutes she was at the doctor's office and taking me to the hospital to see a doctor who specializes in such. At the hospital, I see three different physiatrist who all come to terms that I have major depression and anxiety. If you look at the stat's on LGBTQ, depression, anxiety, are PTSD are very high. Why? Due to the fact that we don't feel accepted, we are trying for so long to hide whoever the true us is, so people don't know.

So again, don't be afraid to seek help. Don't let seeking help scare you. There are many of options out there for us, who will open their ears, doors, and arms to see you be you and help you succeed through it all. Anytime you feel yourself going down, pick up the phone and call the Trevor Project, call a friend, don't try to do it alone.

The Truth of Us, Identity Comparison, my advice to you. These questions that are going to come and go through your head are going to need to be answered. Don't push them back to where you fall deeper and deeper into a dark hole. Answer those questions in your own ways. Keep a journal, make notes of everything, so you can go back a read what has been going through your mind. Personally, for me, music is therapy. If I'm having a bad day, you'll see me with earbuds in listening to music, especially songs that have significant meaning in your life, with my two go to songs being, Strawberries & Cigarettes by Troye Sivan and Keeping a Secret by Bleachers. Keeping a Secret has always had a special place in my heart and it's meaning is so deep to me on a personal level. But everyone has something that makes them comfortable, and to help guide you through this process. If you don't like writing or don't like music, then there must be something for you. Dinner dates with your friends, to help keep everything normal. Family person? Spend quality time with them, again, just to help keep everything normal while you're processing everything. Just remember, be you. That's all you can do.

Parents, this goes back to what I said in section one. Pay attention. When you notice that your child is isolating themselves, try and be there for them. Don't let them go through all of this alone. It goes back to they are going to need you. You may not have all the correct answers for them or know every solution, but just being there, being that wall where they can bounce their feelings off without being judged, just be there. Give a hug and I love you when needed, because those are the two biggest things that make us feel secure. You may not agree, but right now your child is going through something life changing and is needing you. Listen to your child, hear what they have to say, and be there for them. Afterwards, do your homework. Get to understand why your child is going through this.

3

The Truth of Us, Identify Tolerance. This is where people start to begin to accept identifying as gay, lesbian, bisexual, or transgender. Even though they may start accepting to identifying in their way, they still really haven't come out, but maybe to just a couple of people. My tolerance happened in 9th grade when I met a guy. Me and this guy dated from the middle of 9th grade year till about ½ a year after we graduated, due to him moving to Washington State for College and I wasn't ready to leave Alabama yet. We both knew that long distance relationships rarely work, especially when he was out, and he was the only person I was out to at this point.

So, at this point, I have accepted to identify as gay, but I still don't announce it to the world. I'm just not ready for that. I'm identifying as gay and am in love with a guy who treats me perfect, who is also the only one that knows that I am gay. But at this point I am alright with this, because baby steps. As I do identify as gay, it's not like I'm going around shaking people's hand saying, "Hey it's Cody, I'm Gay." That's a negative. It was still pretty much "Hey I'm Cody." I mean just short and sweet and to the point. Plus, why must I continue to constantly announce it to everyone, when in my mind, it was none of their business. I have accepted it, I am happy, and I could care less what people think, nor is it really their business.

I remember the time when I truly had to "identify as gay" and it was a heartbreaking experience for me. Again, I went to a small private school. The blood bank bus was there for donations, and I'm the type of guy that would help anyone out, would give the shirt off of my back to anyone who needs it, or the last $1 to my name, to make sure someone else is happy. So, the chance to give blood, this was important to me. It was a way of helping someone out who truly needed my help. I go onto the bus, they take me back to a room to do questions and to sign my paper work. Simply questions, including "have you been out of the country in the last year". It was all pretty much just basic questions like that. But then came the final question from this nurse, "Have you had sexual intercourse with someone of the same sex?" So, at this point, I'm mortified. I'm thinking to myself, why is this even important? If my blood is no good, you test it before you give it to a new patient, so then you dispose of. I had been tested for HIV and AIDS before because I knew of the risk in the gay community. So, she asked the question, I told her that I had had sexual intercourse with someone of the same sex. Her response to me was, "Well I'm sorry we have policy's in place to where we cannot take blood from gay's." At that point, I just felt my stomach hit my throat. I felt sick. I was a guy that would bend over backwards for anybody and do whatever was needed to help someone out, but here I am being turned away because I was gay. I was pissed non the least, but at that age, it just hurt my feelings. Because then as I'm getting off the bus and classmates realize I haven't given blood, they are asking why? So, I must come up with some lie about my blood sugar was to low for them to risk talking it. They believed that, and all was good. I'm still upset, I go to the parking lot and go to my car and shed a couple of tears because I didn't understand this "rule" that they were trying to explain to me. So, I pulled myself together, went to the office, told the office I needed to use the phone. Who do you call? I called my mom, told her that I felt like I had the stomach flu and I needed to check out. She spoke to the office attendant to give them permission for me to leave. I went home and pretty sure I went straight to researching the reasonings behind why I was asked what I was asked. Again, there are so many safety measures in place in the medical field, that if something is wrong with blood, you'll know before you transfuse it to a new patient. So, don't discriminate to a gay guy, just because sex happens between the same sex.

The Truth of Us, Identify Tolerance, my advice to you. Once you have come to terms to start identifying as gay, lesbian, bisexual, or transgender, if you have a partner, great. You are already out to that one person. Look at two of your friends, the ones that you have known the longest, sit down and have that conversation with them. That way when you have the situation on the blood bank bus that I had, you'll have someone at school who you can talk to, instead of just locking yourself in your car, and ultimately checking out of school. Chances are, if you can identify these friends who you have known for a while, they know. But as your friend, they are not just going to come out and ask you. They want you to be comfortable with coming to them. So, just do it. Will it be awkward? Yes. But the hug and I love you at the end of the conversation makes up for the awkwardness.

Parents, I can't say it enough. Pay attention. Pay attention to who your child is hanging out with. Is your son hanging out with a lot of girls rather than boys his own age? Don't question him on it, but just pay attention. Let him know that you are happy that he has all these friends. He will take notice of you paying attention to him. Just because your child is "identify tolerance" and has made it known to themselves that they are gay, lesbian, bisexual, or transgender, chances are you will not be one of the first people they tell. It's a known fact. Why? Because our parents are our hardest ones to break the news to incase if we let them down. We can handle a friend cutting ties here and there, but family is family. You only get one of those. So, again, pay attention. The more that you pay attention, it will come out better for you in the long run. Trust me!

4

The Truth of Us, Identity Acceptance. This where a person has begun to accept, rather than just tolerate who they are and their sexual identity. You get more comfortable having friendships with other gays, lesbians, transgendered, or bisexual. This is the stage to where your friends began to be told.

I was out of high school before I even hit this part of the journey. But once I told the first person, two more people were told within the same week. Then it was just a couple of people here and there that I had told.

My brother was in Iraq when he found out, but he was totally acceptable of it and has been very supportive thus far. He found out from his wife, my sister n law, which was told in accident.

One night me, my sister n law, and my cousin were all in the car together. We decided we were going to have some vodka to drink that night. I'm not a bring drinker but me and vodka are friends. Not only are me and vodka friends, I'm friends with everyone at the bar. So, anyways we decided to grab a couple of bottles and head home. So, we are all in the same car, and my cousin knows I'm gay, so I text my cousin, and said "Since we are going to be drinking vodka tonight, do you think I should just go ahead and tell my sister n law that I'm gay, so she don't find out from the vodka talking." So, I'm sitting there waiting on my cousins' phone to ding, nothing. But then I hear my sister n laws phone ding. I'm pretty sure I said, "Oh Shit" and just started laughing, because I realized at that time that I had made a major screw up. I was slowly feeling my soul slide out of my ass. She read it and hit me with "there's nothing wrong with that, you are you, and I could care less if your gay or straight." Whew. So, we laughed all the way home about the screw up I managed to do.

I feel that when you hit the acceptance stage, things start changing with you. Nothing bad. But as a gay male, I've noticed on occasion I have what some call the "gay walk", I have a tendency of placing hands on hips when I'm pissed. You just get more comfortable with yourself, and there is not anything wrong with that at all. Be you!

Now with that I will say, as you become more comfortable with yourself, you will see hatred. It's out there in this world and not everyone will be acceptable. It's just one of those things that we must brush off, keep smiling, and just be your wonderful self.

So, I want to tell you another story that happened to me, but first I want to throw out a couple of definitions for you all.

Racism – "prejudice, discrimination, or antagonism directed against someone of a different race based on the belief that one's own race is superior."

Homophobia –" dislike of or prejudice against homosexual people."

In both of these definitions, they mention "prejudice". This is where I want my story to come in, with something that happened to me at Atlanta International Airport onetime.

First and foremost, I would like to say that I am far from a racist. I have best friends who are African-American. I have dated an African-American man, as well as a Latino man. We are all human and that goes back to the way that I was raised growing up in my family.

A few years ago, me, my cousin, and my aunt flew down to Central Florida for a little rest and relaxation. I could only take the weekend off work and they were going to stay for the week. So, my uncle drove down, and then they had a road trip home after the week was up. Well on Sunday, it was time for me to board my plane in Orlando and head to Atlanta International Airport to get my car and drive back to Alabama.

Anybody who knows me, they know that I walk with a mission. I walk 100mph everywhere I go. I get yelled out with anyone who is with me and they all say the same thing "Cody slow down this ain't a race." But that's just me, trying to get where I'm going, quickly.

So, I un-board in Atlanta, being a weekend trip, I just had my rolling carry on bag. I get off the plane and start heading towards the main terminal. Now I respect people inside Atlanta Airport, because I know there are chances of mixed connections, rushing, running, etc. But if I am in your way, please just ask me to move to the side, say excuse me, something.

So, I'm walking and this guy behind me says, "The stupid fucking cracker faggot ass needs to get the fuck out of my way." So, I turn around, I brush it off, and said, "All you had to say was please move."

This was an African-American male, who does not know me, and does not know that I am gay. He is just making assumptions. But in his remarks, he threw out a racial slur at me by calling me a "cracker" and a homophobic slur by calling me a "faggot".

Now, if I wasn't someone who was able of just brushing it off and I threw out a racial comment at him, which one of us would have got the most heat? He would have caused a scene in the airport, requiring security, and I would have been the one who was in Airport Jail. Even though what he said was equally as demining.

The Truth of Us, Identity Acceptance, my advice to you, is accept it. You will be much happier when you do. Yes, the hatred is out there, but there is always far more love. At this point, don't let nothing hold you back from living the life that you want to live. You deserve everything you get in life, and everything that you've got thus far. You've worked hard, possibly years getting to this point, so there is no reason to turn back now. Talk to people, tell people about yourself that you are extremely comfortable with. Enjoy the crowd that you hang around with. Go out and meet more people who are living the same life as you. You would be surprised at what kind of help and information you can get from people who are living the same life as you. You've made it this far! Just keep going. It's the best thing for you.

Parents, again, I apologize, but I can't say it enough. Its just going to come to you paying attention. Notice change in your child's life that it is currently happening. Are they going out more? More LGBTQ friends? Caring more about their appearance? Just pay attention. Make comments (nice) about their new friends and how you are happy they found these people. Chances are with all this attention that you've been paying them, they are ready to come out to you. So, you need to be prepared for that day. Listen to what your child is telling you. Never speak down on them for what they are telling you. Please remember, tell them you love them, hug them. That's all we want. We want to know that you are going to be there for us. We can handle a friend leaving, but family is everything, because you only have one.

5

The Truth of Us, Identity Pride. This is the stage where you take pride in who you are. You will notice yourself out in the gay communities more. Your sexual orientation isn't a big deal at this point. If someone ask, you simply reply with "I'm Gay." It doesn't bother you like it used to.

Everyone gets to different points at different times in their life. My "Pride" moment didn't happen until this year, 2018. I went and watched the movie Love, Simon in theaters, and that was my que. A large part of my people knew me, but not everyone. So, it was time that I just make it official. So, my grand announcement came at 30 years old with a broadcast on Facebook for anyone who possibly didn't know.

Please see the screenshots on the next pages. There wasn't one negative comment made from anyone who knows me. Then I had 2 people message me coming out on their own terms. So, it was a very special moment for me.

I have been MIA from posting on Facebook here recently. It seems like every time you log on, it's some new political crap, with people bickering about nothing. There's still so much hate in this world yet if people would open there eyes more, they would see there's actually more love. There is this new movie that has recently came out called Love,Simon. I went to the theaters to see this movie a total of 3 times. I feel this is one movie that everybody I know should see, no matter what your beliefs are. Within the past month I have had numerous Facebook messages and text messages from people questioning my sexuality. People whom I barely even spoke to in school, people who were older than me in school, and for some reason, they all of a sudden wonder about Cody and what he's about. So to answer the question, yes, I am gay. I wouldn't change a thing about that. I have a mother and father who have shown me nothing but love and support from the moment they were told. I have an older brother and my sister in law, along with my nieces and nephews, that again, show me love and support. Then there's my Emily, one of the first people I ever spoke of about it. She's been my rock through it all. That's what families are for. Not to tear you down when you already feel as if society is not going to accept you. People need to get it together. Families are for love and support, to be there for you, and show you that there is nothing wrong with who you are. My favorite quote from that movie is, "Why is Straight the Default", if there's so much pressure on a gay person to come out, shouldn't a straight person have to? It only makes sense.

Emily Driscoll
I love you BFF !!!!  2

34w   Like   Reply

Bethany Scott Tanner
😍😍😍😍😍 Love it!!!!

34w   Like   Reply   3

Bethany Scott Tanner
You know, the more I think about what you said, it blows my mind that people feel the need to ask you if you're gay. You shouldn't feel like you have to announce to the world that you are. You are you and I am me and that's what makes us who we are. Being gay or straight doesn't define who we are. You are and have always been a beautiful soul and one hell of a hilarious person!!! You'll get nothing but love from me always!! So you just keep being the beautiful bitch we all know you are!! 😘 😘😘

34w   Love   Reply   3

Write a reply...

Beth Kessel McLendon
Ok, now you have made your mom cry first thing in the morning. lol You will never understand how much I love you babe.

34w　Like　Reply　 4

Connie Naramore
Cody Mclendon, you should have done this a long time ago. I'm sure it would have saved you alot of heartache. Love you!!!

34w　Like　Reply　 3

Stephanie Wallace
Um, you forgot about someone who has always known 😊. Love you Cody Mac!

Proud of you today and everyday! 🤍

34w　Like　Reply　 3

Shea Brinegar
I hate it when people have to make PSA. People shouldn't be so nosy. If they are you friends it shouldn't matter. But, I am proud of you for being brave and strong enough to write a PSA.

34w　Like　Reply　 4

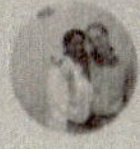
Jessica Sanders
For get them FOOLS U MY MAN

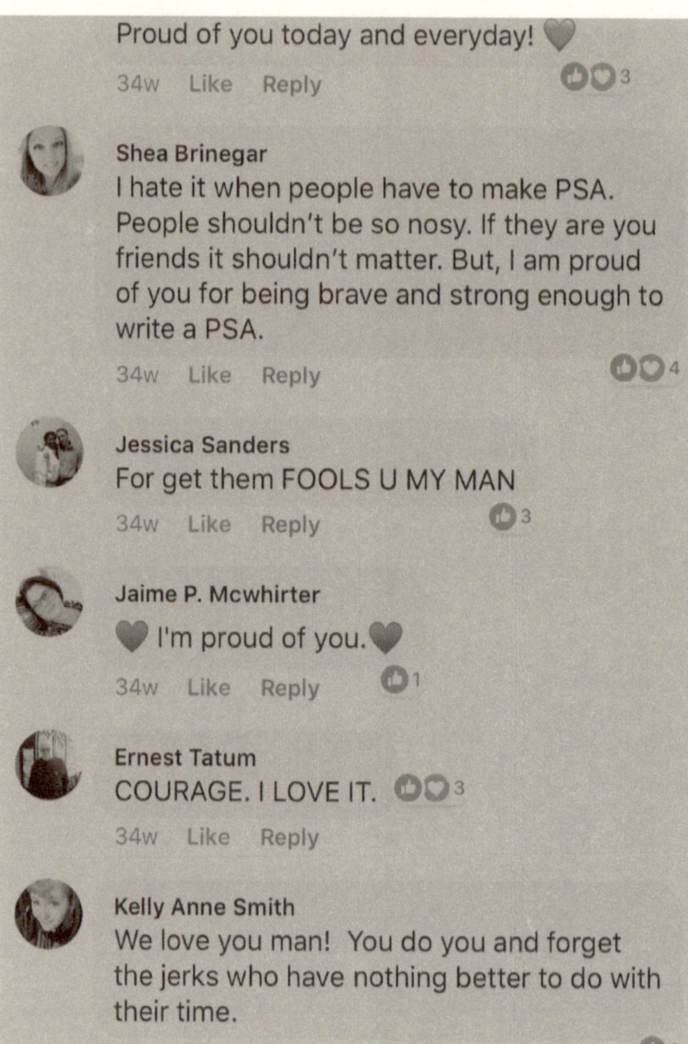

Proud of you today and everyday! 🖤

34w   Like   Reply   3

Shea Brinegar
I hate it when people have to make PSA.
People shouldn't be so nosy. If they are you
friends it shouldn't matter. But, I am proud
of you for being brave and strong enough to
write a PSA.

34w   Like   Reply   4

Jessica Sanders
For get them FOOLS U MY MAN

34w   Like   Reply   3

Jaime P. Mcwhirter
🖤 I'm proud of you. 🖤

34w   Like   Reply   1

Ernest Tatum
COURAGE. I LOVE IT.   3

34w   Like   Reply

Kelly Anne Smith
We love you man! You do you and forget
the jerks who have nothing better to do with
their time.

34w   Like   Reply   1

So, with Identity Pride, this is the biggest step thus far. You've made it and you are proud of who you are. Nobody can take that away from you, they can try, but its up to you to not let them.

The Truth of Us, Identity Pride, my advice for you, be yourself. This is your time to shine. Don't let nothing stop you from what you are capable of doing. This is the biggest milestone in your life that you've created, so embrace it, and don't let anyone steal it. Again, hatred is in this world, learn to smile and brush it off. Kill that hatred with love. That's the best thing to do. As I've said before, if people would just open their eyes a little more, they would see there is a lot more love out there.

Parents, this is it. All that paying attention has paid off. Now just be there for your child. They are about to experience a whole new world and the biggest support system they can have with them is you, their family. Do your homework on the subjects and stand up for what your child believes in. You are their loudest voice and don't ever forget that. They need going through all of this than anytime in the past. All those dirty diaper changes and late-night feedings, well I hope you are in for it again, because you are going to end up being their right hand person and needed more now than ever.

The Truth of Us:

We are human beings that just want to be loved and accepted in this world. We go through a hard time, one that takes us years to figure out who we are. Going through this hard time, we usually do it alone, which usually makes it harder on our bodies and mental state. The Truth of Us is that we are kind and loving people who want to help others and show others love the way that we feel we need to be helped and loved.

The Truth of Us, we can't change who we are. We did not choose to be the way that we are, but once we hit our peak, we wouldn't change a thing about ourselves.

The Truth of Us, we want to be just like you. Normal. We want to go out and have a good time without feeling judged by people who don't even know us.

The Truth of Us, we whole heartily believe that love is love and wish people would quit saying different. Because love is love, no matter who you love, guy, girl, transgender.

That is the truth of us.

Much Love,

Cody McLendon

If you feel yourself in a bind or emergency and just need to talk, go to www.thetrevorproject.org for more information. If it is an emergency, please call them at 1-866-488-7386. This is a 24/7 phone line for those who feel they need someone to talk to.

If you have any questions for me personally, or feel I could give you some advice, please feel free to email me at cody@cmventuresllc.com, and I will make sure to respond to your email.

We are currently working on our second book for the LGBTQ youth, with more stories of myself growing up. It will be a longer book for you to enjoy based off true stories. There will be humor and heart break and everything in between.

Notes:

Notes:

Notes: